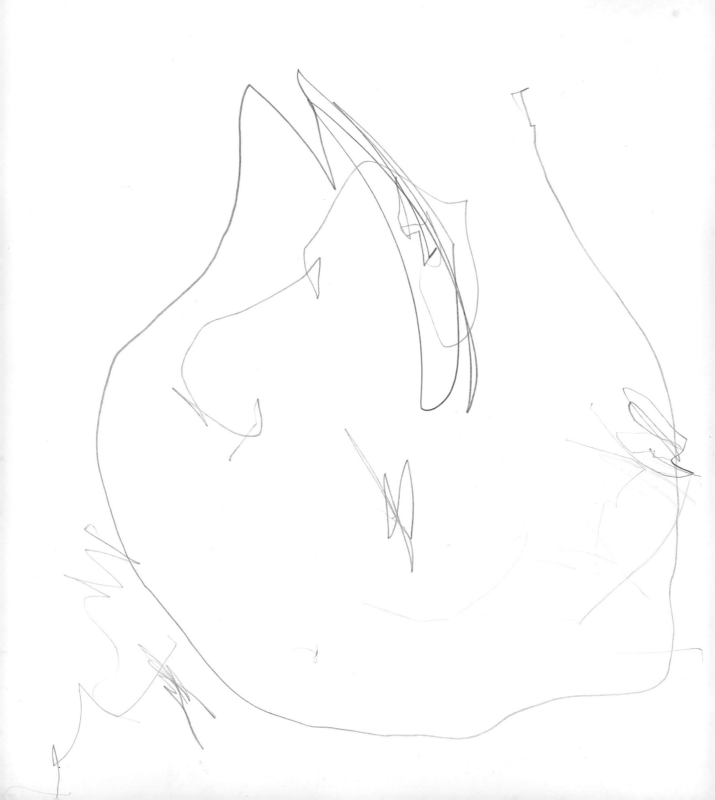

You and Me

We Can Listen

Denise M. Jordan

Heinemann Library
Chicago, Illinois

Customer Service 888-454-2279
Visit our website at www.heinemannlibrary.com

Designed by Sue Emerson, Heinemann Library; Page layout by Que-Net Media™
Printed and bound in China by South China Printing Company Limited
Photo research by Janet Lankford Moran

08 07 06 05 04
10 9 8 7 6 5 4 3 2 1

Library of Congress Cataloging-in-Publication Data
Jordan, Denise.
  We can listen / Denise M. Jordan.
      p. cm. – (You and me)
Summary: Simple text and pictures explain when, where, and why we listen.
  ISBN 1-4034-4408-0 (HC), 1-4034-4414-5 (Pbk)
  1. Listening–Juvenile literature. [1. Listening.] I. Title.
  BF323.L5J67 2003
  153.6'8–dc22

2003012818

Acknowledgments
The author and publishers are grateful to the following for permission to reproduce copyright material:
p. 4 David Pollack/Corbis; p. 5 Mary Kate Denny/PhotoEdit Inc.; pp. 6, 11 Que-Net/Heinemann Library; p. 7 Joe Bator/Corbis; pp. 8, 16, 21 David Young-Wolff/PhotoEdit Inc.; pp. 9, 15 Michael Newman/PhotoEdit Inc.; p. 10 Bill Aron/PhotoEdit Inc.; p. 12 Ariel Skelley/Corbis; p. 13 LWA-Dann Tardif/Corbis; p. 14 Robert Lifson/Heinemann Library; pp. 17, 18 Tony Freeman/PhotoEdit Inc.; p. 19 David Kelly Crow/PhotoEdit Inc.; p. 20 Elena Rooraid/PhotoEdit Inc.; pp. 22, 24 Warling Studios/Heinemann Library; p. 23 (T-B) LWA-Dann Tardif/Corbis, Corbis, David Pollack/Corbis; back cover (L-R) David Pollack/Corbis, LWA-Dann Tardif/Corbis

Cover photograph by Warling Studios/Heinemann Library

Every effort has been made to contact copyright holders of any material reproduced in this book.
Any omissions will be rectified in subsequent printings if notice is given to the publisher.

Special thanks to our advisory panel for their help in the preparation of this book:

Alice Bethke, Library Consultant
Palo Alto, CA

Eileen Day, Preschool Teacher
Chicago, IL

Kathleen Gilbert,
Second Grade Teacher
Round Rock, TX

Sandra Gilbert,
Library Media Specialist
Fiest Elementary School
Houston, TX

Jan Gobeille,
Kindergarten Teacher
Garfield Elementary
Oakland, CA

Angela Leeper,
Educational Consultant
Wake Forest, NC

Some words are shown in bold, **like this.**
You can find them in the picture glossary on page 23.

Contents

What Is Listening?

Listening is **paying attention** to hear something.

When you listen, you are quiet.

You cannot talk and listen at the same time.

When you listen, you think about what you hear.

Where Do You Listen?

You listen when you are at home.

You listen when you are at school.

You listen at the **movie theater,** too.

Wherever you are, you can listen.

When Do You Listen?

You listen to stay safe.

Look and listen for cars before you cross a street.

You listen when you are learning new things.

You can learn how to make pretty art.

What Can You Listen to Inside?

You can listen to a play in a theater.

We are quiet when we listen to a play.

You can listen to a song on the radio.

When we listen, we can learn what the song is about.

What Can You Listen to Outside?

You can listen to your mom teach you how to ride a bike.

You can learn how to pedal.

You can listen to the **coach** teach you how to play the game.

You can learn how to play soccer.

What Can You Listen to at Night?

You can listen to your family.

At dinner, they may tell you how their day went.

You can listen to a bedtime story.

The story may help you go to sleep.

Why Do You Listen?

You listen to get smart.

You learn things when you listen.

When you listen to your parents,
you learn right from wrong.

What Do You See When You Listen?

You see one person talking.

You see other people looking at the person who is talking.

You may see people smiling.

You may see people frowning.

How Do You Feel When You Listen?

You can feel happy when you listen.

It feels good to learn new things.

Quiz

Which group is listening?

Look for the answer on page 24.

Picture Glossary

coach
page 13

movie theater
page 7

paying attention
page 4

Note to Parents and Teachers

Reading for information is an important part of a child's literacy development. Learning begins with a question about something. Help children think of themselves as investigators and researchers by encouraging their questions about the world around them. Each chapter in this book begins with a question. Read the question together. Look at the pictures. Talk about what you think the answer might be. Then read the text to find out if your predictions were correct. Think of other questions you could ask about the topic, and discuss where you might find the answers.

Index

Answer to quiz on page 22

This group is listening.